The Story of the
MAGICAL MYSTERY TOUR

Forward by Alistair Taylor

For almost five years, The Beatles had been the darlings of the critics. John, Paul, George and Ringo could do no wrong – until the first television showing in Britain of *Magical Mystery Tour*. It gave newspapers an opportunity to pan the film which was shown on 26 December 1967, a day known in the UK as Boxing Day. The critics did not pull any punches. They felt that The Beatles had failed, that they had dropped below their usual exceptional standards and that *Magical Mystery Tour* was nothing more than a massive dose of self-indulgence.

Now, thirty years later, the criticism has been shown to have been premature and it may be worthwhile trying to put things into context. In 1967, at the height of psychedelia, *Magical Mystery Tour* was shot in vibrant colour. It was shown on BBC television in monochrome which destroyed so much of the film's impact. The next time you watch it on video turn the colour right down on your television set and this will give you an impression of what the British public saw. It just does not work.

The biggest star of *Magical Mystery Tour* is the music, a fact conveniently overlooked by the critics in their rush to consign the Beatles to history. *MMT* contains some of the boys finest work including the only live performances of "I Am The Walrus" and the spectacular "The Fool On The Hill". Once again, monochrome reduces colourful set pieces to the dullness of dishwater. Yes, the film itself may be flawed but the music certainly isn't.

It is arguable that *Magical Mystery Tour* is far more popular now than in the late Sixties, an argument substantiated by sales of the video. My personal opinion is that it was ahead of its time, something which could be said about so much of The Beatles' output. Certainly, it has many happy memories for me and it was a project which I found myself involved in from the very beginning to the very end – and beyond.

In fact my involvement began with a phone call from Paul one evening in April 1967. This was not uncommon but, on this occasion, Paul was particularly excited. "Come on over to Cavendish Avenue," he said. "I've had this great idea and need your help."

When I arrived, Paul was stretched out on the floor. He was surrounded by several large sheets of paper. On one he had drawn a large circle which he had subdivided into segments. It looked like a bird's eye view of a cake. My curiosity was aroused. "Al, can you remember mystery tours?" he asked.

My mind went back to childhood holidays by the seaside and the coach trips to unknown destinations – mystery tours. Paul continued. "Can you find out if they still do them? Take Lesley and see what you can find out."

"Why?" I asked.

Paul began to tell me that the boys intended making another film which would be based upon a coach trip. However, instead of a courier pointing out the sights, the castles and the tourist attractions, something magical would happen – it would be a MAGICAL mystery tour. He showed me the large sheet of paper with the segments, each segment being an adventure. It was very exciting!

A few days later I took off with my wife, Lesley, for our favourite resort, Eastbourne, on England's south coast. It was a good excuse to get away for a few days and when I returned I was able to tell Paul that mystery tours were alive and well and very popular. "Great!" he said. "Now find me a really brightly coloured coach." So, the following weekend, we trooped off to Eastbourne amidst some of the heaviest rain I have ever seen.

The weather was atrocious. The rain was made worse by high winds which turned the sea into huge, churning waves which crashed against the sea walls. We stayed in the hotel on Sunday morning watching the weather worsen and we decided on an early lunch. I was tucking into roast beef and two veg when a coach pulled into the hotel car park.

I leapt to my feet and began yelling "I've found it! I've found it!" before dashing out into the driving rain, leaving Lesley looking bemused. I stood on the car park, getting drenched, staring at this acid yellow and vicious blue coach. It was perfect.

During the coming months I was kept busy preparing for filming which began on 11 September. The coach journeyed down to Devon and Cornwall but I stayed behind to "mind the shop" and prepare for the sequences to be filmed in Raymond's Revue Bar, a Soho strip club. I had approached the owner, Paul Raymond, when The Beatles suggested the scenes and he was thrilled to help. He had one proviso, we must film early in order that we did not disrupt his regular trade. That seemed fair but there is early and there is early!

We began on Monday 18 September at 6am. That is early! We had problems almost immediately when two representatives of the cinema trades union arrived and threatened to close us down unless we employed the "correct" number of staff. The whole idea of the project was to operate with a minimum crew but these jokers were about to saddle us with thirty two technicians and ancillary staff. We never saw most of them but the rules and regulations stipulated thirty two staff and we had to "employ" thirty two staff if we wanted to finish the film. It was ridiculous!

My outstanding memory from the making of *Magical Mystery Tour* is the sequence featuring "Your Mother Should Know". The scene was Paul's tribute to the American choreographer and film director Busby Berkeley and it was filmed in a "ballroom" which was constructed in a huge aircraft hangar at West Malling Air Base. A sweeping staircase dominated the set and The Beatles rehearsed their entrances on it before disappearing to get changed.

Finally, everything was ready with over 150 members of The Peggy Spencer Formation Dancing Team and a number of Air Force Cadets in position. Then The Beatles appeared at the top of the staircase.

It was incredible!

You could hear the gasps when people first caught sight of them in those white tail suits. Spontaneous applause broke out and cheers rang round the hangar. No one, no one, not even Neil Aspinall or Mal Evans or myself knew anything about the white suits and it was simply breathtaking, a magic, magic moment.

At the end of October, Paul "disappeared". Eventually, it was revealed that he gone to France to film sequences to accompany "The Fool On The Hill". The pictures were terrific and really complemented the song.

When filming eventually ended I thought it was back to normality or what passed for normality in 1967. Wrong! One morning, late in November, John, Paul, George and Ringo strode into my office. They sat on any available surface. They were grinning.

John was the first to speak.
"Al, how about making The Beatles' Christmas Party a *Magical Mystery Tour* Party?"
"Great idea," I said as I tore up the plans for the original party. I expanded the guest list and chose a larger venue and things were falling into place.
Two days later, The Beatles trooped into my office. Once again they were grinning.
This time it was Paul who spoke.
"Al, we have been talking. The Christmas Party. We've decided to include all of the people at Apple. Is it a problem?"
"No," I said, trying to sound casual.
We now had "The Beatles and Apple *Magical Mystery Tour* Christmas Party". I was just wondering how to fit that little lot onto the invitations when George said, "in fancy dress."
I laughed loud and long before I realised that they were serious!

I hired a huge suite at the Royal Lancaster Hotel in Bayswater and it turned out to be a fantastic evening. I went dressed as a matador and Lesley as a Peruvian Princess. Paul and Jane Asher arrived dressed as Pearly King and Queen. And Lennon? He turned up dressed as a rocker, what else? We had a great, great time celebrating, but none of us thought that we would be celebrating still, thirty years on.

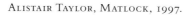

ALISTAIR TAYLOR, MATLOCK, 1997.

THE MAKING OF *MAGICAL MYSTERY TOUR* in the early autumn of 1967 was memorable for me in several ways but mainly because it was the last time I watched The Beatles working together in unison as a friendly group outside the recording studio and genuinely enjoying the gig. They were a bunch of buddies, pals and mates having a fun time. The candid souvenir pictures in this very special book show John, Paul, George and Ringo off-duty and off-guard, proving how relaxed and good-humoured the four boys were as they chatted to fellow actors and fans or posed for snaps during breaks in filming, mingling casually not only with the film's cast members and camera crew but also with passers-by we encountered along the way.

From conception to completion *Magical Mystery Tour* was a unique project. Planned in a great rush only days after Brian Epstein's death, the production was Paul's way of holding the band together at a precarious moment in time when the others, John in particular, had expressed doubts as to whether The Beatles would continue at all without their business manager.

Epstein was found dead on the afternoon of Sunday, August 27, in a darkened bedroom of his luxurious London town house at Chapel Street, Belgravia. Hearing the news in North Wales, where they were on a meditation course with their giggling Indian guru, the diminutive Maharishi, four devastated Beatles made a hurried return to London not knowing quite what was needed or expected of them in such chilling circumstances.

At the age of only 32 years, their flamboyant Liverpudlian mentor and guiding spirit, to whom they gave the affectionate nickname of "Eppy", was the tragic young victim of his own wild yet desperately unhappy personal lifestyle. He took a fatal overdose of booze and drugs during that Bank Holiday weekend while he was too stoned to know what he was swallowing or how much he'd been drinking.

I was surprised to hear from Paul so soon after Brian's appalling accident. He rang to say he was calling a *Magical Mystery Tour* meeting at his North London home in Cavendish Avenue, St John's Wood, for Friday, September 1, and he wanted me round there an hour or two before John, George and Ringo were to join us. Clearly the ideas he had been tossing around in private for several months had now turned into a more urgent enterprise.

In Paul's large cluttered back-room lounge which was where The Beatles often met to make plans or thrash out musical differences, he told me candidly what was on his mind.

Paul said: "If the others clear off to India again now on another meditation trip I think there's a very real danger that we'll never come back together again as a working group. On the other hand, if I can persuade them today that we should go straight into shooting this film, it could save The Beatles."

Paul was looking for my support in gaining the confidence of the others for what was essentially a Paul McCartney project. He hoped to establish his personal reputation as a filmmaker, The Beatles' filmmaker, by handling all aspects of *Magical Mystery Tour* without hiring outsiders to organise things. He saw this as the prelude to a promising new era in the group's career which might otherwise be coming to a premature end.

It was a crazy scheme but a fabulous challenge. Experienced film industry professionals would take months to set up the elaborate production schedule for a feature such as this but Paul wanted us to do it ourselves in a matter of days. He showed me a rough drawing he had done in the shape of a big round clock face, marked out into eight or ten time segments adding up to 60 minutes, each representing a film sequence, some totally blank, a few with suggested songs, others simply saying stuff like "people get on the coach", "magicians in their lab." and "strip club (Soho?)".

I knew the group had recorded a song of Paul's called *Magical Mystery Tour* way back in April and early May but only the barest outline of the film concept had been discussed within the group and even fewer details had reached the rest of us in the small inner circle of business associates and aides surrounding them. In any case, until a notion turned into a reality I never made it my concern — my role in 1967 was that of The Beatles' press and public relations consultant and I preferred to release reliable items of news to the media, not speculative rumours or fictional hype.

Paul told me he had been thinking about *Magical Mystery Tour* for almost a year. After the group's unofficial farewell concert in San Francisco at the end of August 1966 the boys had discussed alternatives to doing live stage shows.

Paul believed they might send out home-made musical and comedy shows occasionally in future to the world's theatres or television stations. This grand-scale global exposure would help to promote their albums and maintain a next-best-thing-to-touring link between The Fab Four and their millions of faithful fans. After all, Paul argued, Elvis had used the cinema and television screens in place of the concert stage so that he could avoid the hassles and pressures of international touring and Paul reckoned The Beatles would have no problem making better and more entertaining movies than The King had done.

Visiting America for the 21st birthday of his long term girlfriend, actress Jane Asher who was working over there in the spring of 1967, Paul had been impressed by a West Coast company of hippy entertainers, the Merry Pranksters, whose outrageously experimental performance fired his enthusiasm for developing *Magical Mystery Tour*. On the homeward flight from the US, Paul wrote most of the show's title song. What would remain undecided for some months was whether The Beatles should aim for a full-blown theatrical film release or, more cautiously, a television special. But if only in Paul's dreams, the production was something that should be seen in the cinema. Much later, after the event and in the wake of bad press reviews, the four boys were to assure the media that *Magical Mystery Tour* was never considered as anything other than TV fare and only a handful of insiders knew differently.

According to Paul, "Eppy" had been put in the picture about *Magical Mystery Tour* within the last week of his life and had reacted very positively but of course his sudden death put a different complexion on everything. When the rest arrived for the Cavendish Avenue summit meeting Paul's now-or-never approach sent an infectious vibration of excitement through all of us in the room. Then John asked quietly: "We can do all this without Brian?" Paul reminded him that Epstein's five-year contract was about to run out and the group had already agreed among themselves that it would not be renewed.

In cold and unemotional business terms, Brian's demise merely advanced inevitable changes which were destined to move responsibility for The Beatles' management from Brian's NEMS Enterprises into their own new self-controlled Apple group of companies. Meanwhile, hand-picked people from NEMS, including some who were earmarked for key jobs within Apple, would pull together all the necessary supporting services to make the immediate production of *Magical Mystery Tour* possible. Somebody would hire a coach and get bright-looking signs designed for the sides. Others would get hold of a professional camera director and a small technical crew to go on the road with the group to the West Country. Paul would take personal charge of auditioning actors and choosing a cast ("although of course we'll all have a say, naturally").

"Why Devon and Cornwall?" I asked during a lull in the conversation. Paul replied: "It's great down there. I went hiking in the west country as a kid. George was with me." And he went back to typing up the meeting's notes with one over-worked index finger of his left hand: "Coach tour (3 days?). Microphone system in coach. Driver, Courier, Hostess - buy uniforms! After coach - Shepperton Studios (one week?)." The sheer enormity of the tasks that lay ahead did not daunt The Beatles. They delegated bits and pieces to those they trusted, ignoring the major fault in the scheme - few of us had the slightest professional experience of film production.

Around this time I can remember raising the question of security and crowd control - how could we expect to take the world's best-known pop band on the road from London to Devon and Cornwall in a brightly painted touring bus without attracting the attention of the press and fans on a grand scale? Paul didn't even pause for thought: "You'll be with us on the bus to look after the press and we'll invite the fan club secretaries who can control their own members if the situation gets out of hand." Other than the group's regular roadies and drivers, we didn't use extra minders or heavies or bouncers to protect the boys.

Perhaps the most remarkable aspect of this whole ill-prepared project was the absence of any shooting script. Paul distributed sheets of paper on which he had put some outline ideas for gags and sketches which might become the basis for film scenes. In each case he had nominated a different Beatle to look after the idea and expand it. Giving one to John he said something like: "Add to it, you know, make more of it if you can. Write some little pieces of dialogue, a few jokes, fill it out whatever way you like. Change it altogether if you've got a better idea. It's all yours."

John was willing to enter into the spontaneity of the occasion but confessed to me: "Writing film lines is nothing like composing song lyrics."

John continued: "I'm not even sure what you need for a script like this. Is this just for us or will the cameramen see it? I'll have to dig out *Help!* and look at that. Have you got a copy if I can't find mine?"

Over the next few days, the Fab Four huddled together to discuss what would be said and done in each scene and this rather crude form of verbal script-writing continued even after we were on the road and filming was well under way. Each of the group got a limited chance to contribute original ideas, although Paul had mapped out what he considered to be the essentials. It was unanimously agreed at the outset that they should try to involve Victor Spinetti, the actor with whom they had formed a friendly rapport during the making of *A Hard Day's Night* and *Help!*. John had already dreamed up a fantasy sequence for himself in which he would play a crazed Italian waiter with heavily-greased hair shovelling heaps of pasta all over an extraordinarily fat lady diner. He was already making mental pictures and chuckling to himself.

Ringo agreed to partner the fat lady, letting her play his auntie. Eccentric Scottish comedy poet Ivor Cutler and the theatrical variety circuit's so-called India Rubber Man, Nat Jackley, were added to the quirky cast as personal nominees of group members. The vast tinsel 'n' sequins Hollywood-type dance finale, to the tune of 'Your Mother Should Know', was Paul's ambitious concoction.

This spectacular scene should have been set at somewhere like Shepperton Film Studios but, unsurprisingly, it was too late to book stage space there or in any of the other studios at short notice. Told of this hiccup, Paul said calmly: "Then we'll hire an RAF aircraft hangar." This was almost precisely what happened and beneath the glittery staircase, beyond the suspended mirror-glass balls and behind the glamourous gowns and white suits worn by some of the 160 dancers, the "ballroom" was actually in the disused shell of a semi-derelict hangar at West Malling Airfield, once an active Second World War USAF base, near Maidstone, Kent.

Costumes for the production's four central characters consisted of outfits in complete contrast to kaftans and other "Summer Of Love" gear The Beatles and the beautiful people of London's "in-crowd" had been seen wearing that year. For the coach trip, the group's film outfits recalled Chicago's legendary gangland heydays. George changed out of a favourite old blue denim jacket and into a big blue suit with black tie. John wore a brown pin-striped suit and feathers in his hat. Paul chose a pullover which was predominantly orange-red while Ringo went along with the "gangster's suit" theme. A contemporary news item in *The Beatles Monthly Book* reported that lots of clothes designers down Carnaby Street were wondering whether The Beatles were about to spark off a nationwide craze for gangster-style Al Capone clothes.

Neil Aspinall, then the group's main roadie since hometown days on Merseyside and now in the nineties the boss of Apple Corps, the London-based machine that still runs The Beatles' ongoing business empire, nutshelled the informality of the *Magical Mystery Tour* venture when he said later without gross exaggeration: "We went out to make a film and nobody had the vaguest idea of what it was all about." No wonder one critic called the finished product "the most expensive home movie the world has ever seen".

Paul had a nostalgic reason for choosing Allsop Place, the small street beside Tussaud's and the London Planetarium, as the pick-up spot where we would join the *Magical Mystery Tour* bus. This was traditionally the departure point where pop stars and their bands gathered at the beginning of cross-country concert tours in the Sixties. In early days, Paul and the others had waited there for buses laid on by concert tour promoter Arthur Howes.

At ten thirty on the morning of Monday, September 11, we turned up to find that most of the professional actors and fan club "extras" had arrived early although our bus had not. Paul smiled patiently and kept his cool: "I just know we got this coach through Arthur didn't we?" He passed the waiting time chatting to his fellow "tour passengers" and taking the fan club secretaries for a cup of tea in a handy London Transport canteen generally reserved for staff.

Two hours later than our scheduled set-off time the big yellow and blue bus, hired from a coach firm in Hayes, just like the concert tour ones, eventually pulled away with 43 people on board including half a dozen hired technicians. The delay was blamed on the flimsy paper used for the hastily painted *Magical Mystery Tour* posters which wouldn't stick to the outside of the bus because of the windy and wet weather that morning. A watching crowd of newspaper photographers and reporters from Fleet Street raced off to their parked cars and drove after us in hot pursuit. Somewhere on the A30 near Virginia Water we picked up John, George and Ringo at a point on our route which was closest to their Surrey homes.

Then we were on our way. I remember thinking how incredible it was that this world-class supergroup should be sitting on a bus chatting away so nonchalantly and contentedly to teenage fans whose friends would have given an arm or a leg to spend this mind-blowing week in the close-quarters company of their fave pop idols.

Would Elvis or even Cliff have treated their fans to such a gob-smacking summer holiday outing even if the girls were doubling as useful film extras? Three different Area Secretaries of The Official Beatles Fan Club from the home counties were chosen to join National Secretary Freda Kelly on the bus because they were fastest at phoning her back after getting a telegram from me.

Sylvia Nightingale from Sussex, Barbara King from Essex and Jeni Crowley from London got to know The Beatles pretty well during the course of week's travelling and the filming. They ate with the boys, sat beside them on the bus and socialised generally with the rest of us in the evenings. Each one took away memories to last a lifetime. Jeni did an emergency sewing job for John. She told me: "The buttons had come off the back of his trousers. He needed them because he was wearing braces. Jokingly, I offered to sew them on. It would have been easier if he hadn't been wearing them at the time!" One of Barbara's lingering memories was of lunching beside John, Paul, George and Ringo at a steak bar in Plymouth: "I remember how rude people were, persistently bothering the four lads while they were trying to eat." The Beatles were impressed by what Sylvia wore: "I decided on hippy gear for the trip and The Beatles constantly referred to me as Zippy Hippy and Miss Freak Out. As I ate lunch to the jingle of my bells, John turned to me and said 'You younger generation with all your bells!' Later, at a little place called Bodmin I was given an orange lolly ice and Ringo was sucking a red one. 'Do you want to swap?' he said. 'It's quite clean, I've licked it all over for you!'"

Liverpool-based Freda Kelly, one of the group's earliest fan club organisers was the only one already well-acquainted with the lads, having known them since Cavern Club days but even Freda had been stunned when I rang a few days earlier.

I asked if she could take time off from sorting through her mountains of fan mail to join the boys for a week. "It was a marvellous surprise," she told me later. She was also surprised that The Beatles personally organised events on the bus: "Before starting to film, the boys moved people around and asked us to keep our new seats all the time so that whenever we happened to be in camera range we'd be seen in the same part of the bus. What's more we were to wear the same clothes all through the week — which created washing problems as the days went by!" Freda was moved up from the back of the coach and Paul came over to her for a chat. She told me: "He handed me a box of Maltesers and said 'Have these for a slim figure like yours'. We stopped at a restaurant called The Pied Piper for lunch. The boys got their meals in no time, staff being overwhelmed to find such distinguished customers arriving unexpectedly. Some of us still hadn't got our orders when the lads were on their second course. George looked over and asked why we were still waiting. Then he went into the kitchen and emerged a moment later with my lunch."

With no proper shooting script for guidance, the camera crew were given the brief: "If in doubt, film it." Not only Freda and her several Fan Club Area Secretaries but most of the actors were never too sure what was real and what was set up as a scene for the film. Was this stop at a chip shop a necessary meal break or another carefully plotted film scene? Was the chance to swim in a hotel pool simply a bonus or another camera opportunity? Was this a group of fans or hired extras waving at the bus?

the line between fact and fiction became increasingly blurred in their minds as the week went on. The boys tended to add to the confusion by wearing their "fancy dress" character costumes most of the time because (a) there was nowhere to change in private on the bus and (b) they might decide at any moment to do some more filming.

Each morning The Beatles held some sort of informal planning meeting to sort out the day's work. Cold and wet weather and other problems, including the intrusion of fans, meant that we seldom kept to our agreed schedule. On the second day, for example, we didn't go to our pre-arranged location because the bus was too big to cross a narrow bridge and we were forced to turn back, creating a major rural traffic jam in the process. When we reached the seaside at Newquay, we established our base for three nights at the cliff-top Atlantic Hotel where the cameramen generally split into separate units so that two scenes could be shot simultaneously at different spots. Among other things, the Wednesday was earmarked for Paul to direct a scene on the bus with Ringo, his Auntie (actress Jessie Robins) and Mr Buster Bloodvessel (Ivor Cutler) while John took charge of Happy Nat (Rubber Man) Jackley's big slapstick scene in which he would dream about chasing young girls round a swimming pool causing all kinds of mayhem and hilarity.

Fan club secretaries who happened to have brought suitably brief swimwear in their baggage and recently recruited local girls shivering a little in their bikinis were joined at the pool by the obliging female partners of one or two Fleet Street reporters who had fetched them down from London for the ride. As John, comfortably wrapped up in a warm sheepskin-lined jacket, gave everyone last minute instructions and told his camera director what he wanted, the line-up of poor near-naked girls nursed their hardening goosebumps and huddled in a row against a brick wall which scarcely sheltered them from the bite of a chilly sea breeze.

It wasn't all good fun, you see, well not for the girls anyway. And not for Happy Nat Jackley either as it turned out. Unfortunately for the veteran comedy actor and through absolutely no fault in Jackley's brilliantly daft performance, The Beatles later decided to scrap John's entire poolside footage which finished on a cutting room floor in Soho rather than on the world's TV screens. Only one of the bikini girls, one we had nicknamed The Lovely Linda, survived the editor's scissors to make a blink-and-you-miss-her split-second appearance elsewhere in the finished product waving from a tower window. Inevitably other sequences suffered a similar fate when ten hours of film had to be cut ruthlessly to less than 60 minutes. One was a scene where George sat in his big blue jacket meditating deeply in the middle of a cornfield.

Considerable time had been spent in locating a suitably remote meadow but hordes of well-wishers and media reporters turned up anyway. Also cut was a big lunch filmed in the hotel to ballroom dance band accompaniment. It simply didn't work when the boys looked at it later in the cold light of a cutting room.

But it was the BBC, not The Beatles' who deleted another element of that Wednesday's busy shooting schedule, a romantic tongue-in-cheek beach scene between eccentric Buster Bloodvessel and Auntie Jessie which Paul had filmed. Somebody at the Beeb felt it was in bad taste and not fit for family yuletide viewing. For such reasons the version of the *Magical Mystery Tour* story depicted in the strip cartoon pages which formed part of the soundtrack EP record packaging differed in various details from that first seen by BBC television viewers over the following Christmas and New Year period.

Sometimes the large crowds of onlookers and national press people who stalked The Beatles everywhere came in handy. When we wanted to shoot as large a crowd of people as possible with The Beatles outside the Atlantic Hotel, members of the public were invited to join in and wave along as the cameras rolled. Eagle-eyed observers might later spot celebrity visitors among the crowd including musician Spencer Davis who was holidaying in the area and threw a farewell party for the boys before we headed back to London on the Friday morning.

We left behind in the West Country one massively delighted Taunton chip shop owner, a Mrs Amy Smedley, who had a surprise visit by The Fab Four and told her local paper: "They got here at lunchtime and shot some film outside our shop. Then all four came inside to have some fish and chips. I still can't really believe they actually ate my fish and chips." Dave Hale, a passenger on the bus recalls, "On the way back just like a real coach trip, they called in on the fish and chip shop in Roman Road, where everybody ate. Everyone spilled out of the coach in this nearly empty housing estate with just a few people looking curiously on. By the time they came out of the shop, the word had spread like wildfire and the coach was surrounded by local people. The Beatles were always very pleasant and patient, signing autographs."

Several other local shopkeepers and pub licensees had similarly special tales to tell and treasure after we'd gone. And most people on the bus had special memories of their own to take home, not only of the week's film work but of leisure evenings socialising with The Fab Four, perhaps a bar-parlour piano sing-song led by Paul, maybe a pair of ciggies smoked with George or a personal secret shared with John, a game of pool with Paul or a pint of bitter with Ringo.

Although filming was far from finished when our coach pulled out of Newquay, there was a bitter-sweet end-of-term feeling among the "passengers", as if the magic might soon wear off and the bus would turn back into a pumpkin. On the journey home we drank bottles of beer and sang seaside coach trip songs as dusk fell and the first suburban London landmarks came into sight. Most people on the bus, even the amateurs, had become so accustomed to film work that few even noticed the professional accordionist (Shirley Evans) who accompanied our singing, the occasional clatter of the clapper board or the dazzling camera lights that kept coming on and going off.

Far from taking a weekend break, The Beatles booked themselves into

EMI's Abbey Road studios on the Saturday night to work on Paul's 'Your Mother Should Know', John's 'I Am The Walrus' and George's 'Blue Jay Way', each of which required finishing touches.

The next scene to be shot, on Monday 18 September, involved a guest appearance by The Beatles mates "Legs" Larry Smith, Vivian Stanshall and their zany Bonzo Dog Doo Dah Band who would sing 'Death Cab For Cutie' in a strip club setting. Larry Smith recalls, "We were doing cabaret up in the north of England, and our roadie came rushing back from the telephone and said, 'you're not going to believe this.' The Beatles had personally asked us to perform." This sequence was eventually slotted into the previous week's action so that it looked as if The Beatles and a few of

the other men on the *Magical Mystery Tour* coach had sneaked off to a sleazy club for a naughty night out.

The general office manager of NEMS Enterprises and former assistant to Brian Epstein in his Liverpool record-retailing days, Alistair Taylor, nicknamed "Mr Fixit" because of his ability to handle seemingly impossible tasks for the Fab Four, had the job of finding a place for the striptease filming. Paul Raymond, publicity-minded boss of Raymond's Revuebar, was a good friend of his: "When I told him we needed a stripper he suggested we use his place." Raymond arranged for the Revuebar's popular Jan Carson to do a toned-down version of her strip act for the cameras on the stage as the Bonzo Band performed behind her. Alistair's assistant, Tony Bramwell, remembers being asked "to book strippers for a sequence to be filmed in the Raymond Revuebar and I have a vivid recollection of spending most of an afternoon watching one particular girl take her clothes off time and time again while the Bonzos played and John and George sat there ogling her."

During the shoot, Alistair found himself having to deal with an awkward and unexpected visit by trade union representatives who told him: "If you carry on without a full crew, Mr Taylor, we shall black the film". They wanted to saddle The Beatles with a film crew five times larger and more expensive than was needed. Taylor reported afterwards: "They were as immovable as boulders. I had to admit defeat. I'm glad I'm not a Mr Fixit in the film business!" The tensions of this stressful night were added to by the theft of the band's instruments from an alley behind the Revuebar. Replacement saxes and drum kit had to be rushed to the scene. Months later when *Magical Mystery Tour* went on sale to foreign broadcasters, further bad luck was in store for the Bonzos. Despite the toning down of Ms Carson's sexy but tasteful striptease, Hong Kong television station executives cut her scene and, consequently, the entertaining musical contribution of Stanshall, Smith & Co., deeming all this stuff to be much too risqué for sensitive Asian viewers.

The following week at West Malling proved to be more productive and less unpredictable than the West Country. For one thing the airfield was not accessible to the public so there were no distractions and crowd control was no longer a problem.

Inside the sprawling site's huge Hangar 3 a whole range of scenes were shot in record time including the Magicians' Laboratory sequence, for which The Beatles donned tall pointed hats and cast spells over bubbling glassware, Auntie Jessie's Dream, in which John fulfiled a masochistic fantasy by smothering the unfortunate woman in spaghetti, and George's mysterious 'Blue Jay Way' song, where he was seen singing and playing in a re-creation of the swirling smog found in the Los Angeles of the sixties. In this work-intensive five-day period we also completed the farcical army recruitment office scene, featuring "Major McCartney" with the marvellous Victor Spinetti as his Sergeant, the wacky marathon races which were done on the airfield runway and perimeter roads, and the innovative "video clip" for John's bizarre 'I Am A Walrus', a trend-setting sequence which showed off the extraordinary song to mind-boggling visual and audio advantage.

Finally, on Sunday, September 24, came the spectacular ballroom scene for 'Your Mother Should Know', involving two dozen youthful cadets from a local squadron of the Women's Royal Air Force plus 160 members of Peggy Spencer's formation dance groups, The Beatles, alternately in pristine white ties and tails and their magician outfits, with the rest of the company spread around them in hastily choreographed array.

The physical and mental logistics of assembling, placing precisely and then shifting around this amazingly large company in time to The Beatles' music presented crowd control problems that made Newquay seem quite tame in retrospective comparison.

Remarkably everything that was needed went "in the can" that day and it was almost a wrap on The Beatles' first and last DIY music and comedy film. All that remained was a short agenda of "add on" scenes to link the rest, but these needed only the boys themselves plus other selected central characters.

One of the final scenes to be shot was Paul's 'The Fool On The Hill', for which he and a small crew flew to the south of France at the end of October. Tony Bramwell recalls, "It was realised that nothing had been shot for 'Fool On The Hill' so Paul set off for France one day going back to a hill above Nice which he'd seen on a previous visit. Of course, because The Beatles had become so used to operating with assistants and minders, it never occurred to him to take his passport. Usually someone else would do that for him. When he got to customs he told them his passport was already in France, and when he got to France he told them it was following on from England. I think they were only too happy to let him in." Beatles assistant Peter Brown estimated that, "by the time Paul and the crew returned to London, it had cost £4,000 just for the one shot of him sitting on the hill." An additional garden sequence for 'Blue Jay Way' showing George and the others playing a white cello on top of a rockery was filmed on Friday 3 November. People have always assumed that since 'Blue Jay Way' was George's song the garden setting was at his house in Esher. In fact the picturesque garden at the back of Ringo's place in Weybridge was used for the filming and fireworks originally intended for Guy Fawkes Night were let off to provide the cameras with a colourful conclusion to the scene.

Although Paul said he intended to stick around in London to follow through on all the intricate final stages of the film's post-production process, the others were itching to take off for India at the renewed invitation of the Maharishi Mahesh Yogi.

Paul had initially allowed one week for editing but the work of cutting and assembling the finished film, plus the completion of the six soundtrack recordings, took substantially longer. Eventually, realising how much work still had to be done on the recordings, John, George and Ringo also delayed their next spell of Transcendental Meditation and put back their trip to India until the new year.

Meanwhile, the boys had locked themselves away in recording studio mixing suites and film editing rooms for hours on end making sure that scenes for which each one had accepted personal responsibility would finish up the way they wanted. The editing process began on the 25th September at Norman's Film Productions in Old Compton Street, Soho, London and lasted for several weeks. The Beatles employed Roy Benson to edit the film. From all accounts it was a friendly but chaotic atmosphere in Old Compton Street. Norrie Drummond, the *New Musical Express* journalist, remembers," the room was hot and smoky. Long strips of film hung from steel coat racks and dozens of LPs lay scattered around the floor. Empty coffee cups were dotted everywhere and ashtrays spilled over with cigarette butts. John and Ringo were sitting on a table watching the film through a viewfinder, while Paul was synchronising the sound of a barrel organ". John Lennon's school friend, Pete Shotton, dropped in one afternoon and found John "in a particularly good mood. He even called out the window to an elderly drunk we heard singing in the street, and invited him to join us. The drunk duly shambled upstairs, bottle in hand, to lead John, Paul, George and Ringo through a round of old drinking songs such as There's An Old Mill By The Stream. He seemed totally oblivious to the identity of his new friends."

My function at this stage was to compile and write the little story book to go with the recordings. This consisted of photographic "stills" done by John Kelly during the filming together with a strip cartoon drawn by Bob Gibson giving a boiled-down version of the *Magical Mystery Tour* film story.

I was pleasantly surprised by the amount of personal time Paul gave to working with me on the cartoon captioning and the rest of the booklet. Having been handed the job of editor, I imagined I would be left alone to get on with it but Paul was in and out at all hours of the day to offer comments and suggestions: "Let's put the words 'wonderful spells' in capital letters, shall we." "Can Bob do little drawings to go across the top of each page, do you think?" "I love the way he's drawn the magicians."

As I indicated earlier, the printing of the booklet had to meet EMI's production deadline for a (December 8) UK record release date so the cartoon story included snatches of storyline not seen in the final edit of the actual film – we were unable to wait and see what would be cut and what would be left in.

For America, we had to meet the record company's even earlier deadline for a November 27 release, Incidentally, for the US, Capitol Records added five extra numbers not featured in the film at all, including 'Penny Lane', 'Strawbery Fields' and 'All You Need Is Love', and issued the collection as a full-length 12-inch LP record rather than a 7-inch extended player.

BBC Television presented the Boxing Day premiere screening of *Magical Mystery Tour*, transmitted in black and white on BBC-1, and sandwiched in a primetime mid-evening 52-minutes slot between (David) *Frost Over Christmas* and Norman Wisdom in *The Square Peg*. They expected it to draw 20 million viewers, the eventual figure was 13 million, reportedly one million less than David Frost.

A considerably smaller BBC-2 audience watched the show in colour a couple of weeks later. No longterm damage was done to The Beatles' record sales by the spread of decidedly negative media reviews which the film attracted at the time. Indeed as years passed an increasing number of critics and fans agreed that the often bizarre humour of *Magical Mystery Tour* contained elements of Pythonesque comic genius and the whole production may have been some years ahead of its time.

TONY BARROW

ATLANTIC HOTEL

The Beatles arrive at the Atlantic Hotel, Newquay 12th September 1967.

GEORGE SPEAKS TO MIRANDA WARD OUTSIDE THE ATLANTIC HOTEL.

"Paul, I suppose, had the original idea. It all started with a song that he wrote called Magical Mystery Tour, which we recorded shortly after Sgt. Pepper. Then the idea came that the TV show we wanted to do could be built round it.

It's a typical coach tour except that it's called the Magical Mystery Tour - so anything can happen in it!

This part that we are doing now is mainly just to tie the whole show together - the links. Because it's magic we can do anything - let our ideas run riot!

These parts - sequences - we just have a few ideas - are mainly to show the people getting on and off the bus and a few little things that occur during the course of a coach trip.

Most of the work will start next week when we go into the studios to do the scenes that'll go between the location sequences.

We want everyone who watches to be able to freak-out as it were - but we don't want to frighten them. Some people get a bit frightened when the music suddenly goes strange as in Day In The Life because they don't know what's happening.

In this film we don't want the viewer to be puzzled or scared. We will be able to freak them out a little bit - our excuse will be that it's a magical mystery tour - so everyone will be calm. They expect anything to happen when magic is involved!

The title song will be played over the beginning when all the party are boarding the coach - the other numbers will be incorporated into the fantasy or dream sequences between the coach party scenes.

The courier, say, will ask everybody to look to their left some old building or local landmark; then to look to their right ..... and they'll see it that's where the material we shoot in the studios will come in!"

George and I were sitting on the grass outside our hotel in Newquay, Cornwall, over cups of tea. "The only place where I get good tea is at home!" he commented, as he poured.

"It's sad really because some of our staunchest fans are the ones who will never get to know us, just because of the way they act. We are obviously not going to hang around when they are screaming, shouting and trying to pull our clothes off! It's the quiet shy ones who we get chance to chat to," he explained as he signed autographs and poured yet more cups of tea.

George being interviewed by Miranda Ward 13th September.

Wednesday lunchtime

After waiting for about 30 minutes for my favourite Beatle, John appeared at the main entrance dressed in a white roll neck sweater. He walked out very casually and strolled over towards where we stood. We approached John and asked for his autograph, to which he replied, "Sorry, luv, not today". Shell-shocked at meeting my favourite Beatle I quietly asked, "What's the film about?" He replied, with a slight grin, "I haven't got a clue, the gaffer's coming out in a minute, try asking him." My sister asked, "Do you like Newquay?" and John replied "Yeah, it's really nice. Do you live here?" We said we didn't live far away and then John casually strolled to the edge of the forecourt and stood looking at the magnificent view over Newquay Bay. Then he walked back inside. Not long after Paul came out and everyone rushed to him, 40 or 50 fans had assembled by now. Paul happily chatted and signed autographs and in the meantime Ringo appeared and he too signed a few things. Then Paul and Ringo got on the coach and it set off on a trip through the narrow Newquay streets with about fifteen cars in hot pursuit! - Phil Rouse, Newquay Beatle fan who photographed The Beatles (above) before they set off for Wednesday afternoon's filming.

A kaftan-clad Paul trudges along Tregurrian beach during Wednesday afternoon's filming.

Ivor Cutler (humorist/poet):

I had done a TV show, Late Night Line Up, and McCartney saw it. He saw what I was singing and became fascinated with the harmonic structure and came to see me. It was some months afterwards that I was asked to do The Mystery Tour. I asked why and I was told that Paul and John, in particular, respected me and liked my work.

The character I played was called Buster Bloodvessel. They filmed a sequence on Tregurrian Beach where I had a romantic interlude with Jessie Robins who played Aunt Jessie. I rather enjoyed it but the BBC censored it. They cut it out when the film was shown. Maybe they felt that people of our age had no business to be doing that sort of thing.

I don't think Ringo was very sure of me. He was an easy-going kind of bloke, but I'm not much use in those kind of situations. You either take me or leave me. George was similar but less intense. He was into the Maharishi at that time and I'm no good at things like Zen.

Paul seemed a very intelligent, shrewd man. His mind was really keen, very much a seeker after information, very aware and alive but always with a mind rather like a machine in some ways, busy synthesising and correlating all the time. That's not a criticism.

John was the one I found easiest to get along with. I suspect it was mutual.

In the afternoon Paul and Ringo went off again in the coach whilst John and George directed scenes by the hotel. At least John did mainly with George throwing in the odd suggestion. John sent me off to buy a bathing dress so that I could be included in the swimming pool sequence. I got out of it, though, by escaping to the warmth of the hotel for more tea with George, after which we retired to the peace and quiet of his room to do the interview for Radio One's Scene & Heard.

After dinner that evening Ringo and I played table tennis against road-manager Neil Aspinall and a friend. Unfortunately, they won! This was due to the fact that I'm not very good at ping-pong and Ringo was rather restricted in movement after making one very brave attempt to save the game and splitting his trousers! "That's the end of having velvet trousers made from curtain material."

After losing about five games we went upstairs to play bar billiards. We were joined by Spencer Davis.

Spencer was on holiday with his family a few miles down the coast and dropped in to say hello.

In a mad fit of enthusiasm at being bedside the sea, and because I had missed the swimming pool sequences, I decided to have a late night swim! Neil came down to watch over me and then plied me with brandies afterwards! Well I couldn't go to the seaside and not swim, could I?" –MIRANDA WARD (JOURNALIST).

"John shouted directions while the camera team sweated and toiled, and the girls jumped into the freezing pool of Atlantic water. George protected himself from the chill Newquay breezes in a blue denim jacket and watched approvingly while the girls leapt around, their skin getting bluer by the minute, trying to look happy and carefree." – CHRIS WELCH, MELODY MAKER JOURNALIST *commenting on the filming of the sequence directed by John Lennon in which Happy Nat The Rubber Man (Nat Jackley) chased young women around the Atlantic Hotel's outdoor swimming pool.*

JUDITH ROGERS, LOCAL SCHOOLGIRL, "When we heard that The Beatles were in Newquay, my friend, Julie, and I decided to skive off school and hang around the Atlantic Hotel. We were amazed because one of their crew came up and asked us if we'd like to be in the film. On Tuesday afternoon we were filmed around the pool at the back of the Atlantic Hotel, it was funny because we were in bikinis and The Beatles all had these long Afghan coats on! Later in the afternoon we went up to film at Huer's Hut, a sort of fisherman's look-out point on top of the cliffs behind the hotel. George Harrison was supposed to come into the hut pick me up and put me on a ledge ……..God knows why!………and I remember thinking I'm being picked up by a Beatle! My friend Julie and I had a cine camera and The Beatles started dancing around in front of it posing with us and acting daft.

Later that day we were picked up in a car and driven to Fistral Beach. It was just Paul, myself, my friend Julie, her parents and younger brother. Paul was looking for new places to film. It was really nice, the sun had just set and we had found a place with lots of rocks. We all just chatted and walked. We were taken home later that night in a private car.

Julie and I were asked to go back to the hotel the next morning and I ended up sitting in George Harrison's lap in the foyer for about half an hour. He told me how much he hated being followed and chased everywhere by fans because it was scary. He said he was happy to talk to fans for as long as they wanted if they just wouldn't scream all the time. I was just sat there.. loving every minute of it! Later that afternoon we had lunch in the hotel, with Spencer Davis and a lot of other people. I remember a foreign looking man who always wore white jeans (Magic Alex) he used to hang around the hotel and chat to the local lads."

Paul signing for an attractive MMT extra inside the Atlantic.

Thursday morning 14 September, the story of The Magical Mystery Tour continues with The Beatles setting out from the Atlantic Hotel to find a meadow in which they can film George meditating. Despite the crowds of onlookers and umpteen cars following them they eventually locate a field not far from Newquay. In addition to George's sequence, which did not find its way into the end product, The Beatles also filmed the scene in which all the passengers from the bus crowded into a small tent. In the finished version this turns into a small theatre in which the Blue Jay Way sequence is shown.

MIRANDA WARD: *After lunch the sound-crew had to go back to London and Paul asked me to help out. Armed with my tape-recorder I followed him round the field switching on the mike when directed.*

The Beatles pictured inside the Atlantic Hotel, Thursday 14th September.

NICOLA HALE (Passenger, known as Little Nicola in the film) : *"I have a vivid memory of fighting with Paul McCartney on the floor of the hotel, and playing table football with Ringo Starr and John Lennon. I remember John asking my mother for sixpence."*

Dave Hale (bus passenger) : *"My mother-in-law expected everyone to be strange and weird but The Beatles were always nice and polite. In the evenings John or Paul played piano and led everyone in sing-songs. John hadn't brought enough underpants for the week and so Pam's mother bought him some. Nicky was more interested in the cameras than in The Beatles."*

Freda Kelly : *"We were all filmed during lunch one day. Apparently The Beatles had been in the ballroom the night before having a drink and got chatting to this bandleader chap. Paul asked him what he was doing for lunch the next day and when he said 'Nothing,' he was recruited to play while we ate."*

Spencer Davis : *"The Spencer Davis Group had just finished a tour and I was having a holiday, staying with my wife and daughters at the Tywarnhale pub in Perranporth, which was owned by the parents of our roadie, Alec Leslie. I knew The Beatles quite well, so when I heard that they were filming at the Atlantic Hotel in Newquay I called up and asked Mal Evans what was going on.*

Mal immediately invited me over, so the whole family got into the Mini and drove over there. Paul seemed to be directing the filming and, to my amazement, one of the film crew turned out to be John Mayall's wife Pamela. We were immediately roped in to do a bit of filming and you can see us in a group shot at the back of the bus, which also appears on the back cover of the album.

While we were chatting during the day, I invited Paul back to the pub in Perranporth for a drink. So that night, I'm sitting in the bar when in walks Paul and Ringo. The punters in the pub just couldn't believe it. Paul, being the sort of character he is, just grins at everybody, shouts out 'Evening all,' and then installs himself at the piano, where he sat belting out pub songs all evening with everybody singing along until about two in the morning. That was such a great night."

The ATLANTIC HOTEL
NEWQUAY

Menu

"........usually they were always in a rush but on this occasion the four of them were standing in front of the reception desk so I picked up the nearest piece of paper to hand, which was the Atlantic Hotel menu card and asked them for their signatures......." MISS DAVIS, ATLANTIC HOTEL RECEPTIONIST.

Annabelle Pascoe, daughter of the proprietor of the Atlantic Hotel : *"I was sixteen at the time and my parents owned the Atlantic Hotel. They didn't tell me they were expecting The Beatles, so on my way home from school I saw what looked like hundreds of these girls running around on the lawn and I couldn't understand it.*

The hotel was full so The Beatles stayed in our annexe which is across the car park and over a little bridge, which also gave them a bit more privacy and allowed them each to have a room of their own.

This wasn't long after Brian Epstein had died, and I remember that they still had a lot of letters of condolence arriving every day. Most of them ended up in the waste paper bins.

The whole time they stayed we had to have the curtains on the ground floor drawn, because otherwise there would be girls staring in through all the windows.

At lunchtime the next day we had a dinner party in the ballroom which was filmed and you can see The Beatles being served by our waiters on the inside cover of the Magical Mystery Tour EP.

We had a little three piece band with a violin, piano and drums, and all four of The Beatles danced waltzes and fox-trots to their music with the hotel residents, most of whom would have been in their fifties.

The Beatles were the biggest thing ever in those days and I was incredibly excited but I was also much too shy to go up to them so in the end my dad had to drag me over, I shook hands with Paul McCartney and he said 'What are you grinning at?' I went bright red all over.

They wore the same clothes for the whole time they were with us, which I suppose was for continuity in the film, but after they'd booked out we found Paul McCartney had left a pair of underpants in his bed!"

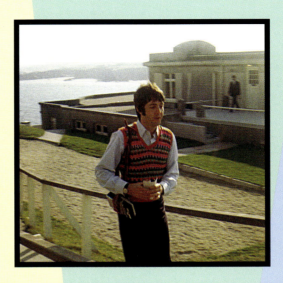

Leaving the Atlantic Hotel on the 15th September.

West Malling 19th-24th September

WEST MALLING

The filming of The Magical Mystery Tour continued on Tuesday 19th September. The Beatles hired West Malling Air Station for one week and filmed inside a large empty hangar. The scenes filmed at West Malling included the Magicians Laboratory, Aunt Jessica's Dream, George's 'Blue Jay' Way, the Major McCartney sequence plus the 'Your Mother Should Know' finale. Some scenes were shot outside the hangar and these included the 'Marathon', The 'Tug of War', 'I Am The Walrus' and the newsagency sequence.

Stan Brown still remembers that day in September 1967. The former West Malling newsagent then had his shop on the opposite side of the High Street. It was a warm Saturday afternoon and he was serving behind the counter of the Town Newsagency when the producer of the film called round, asking if he could "borrow" the shop. He wanted to shoot a scene which required a booking office for tickets for the Magical Mystery Tour. "I said no, I still had half an hour's business time left - it was only 5 o'clock - but that they could use it after 5.30." Word of The Beatles' visit had already spread around town and by 5.30 pm crowds had gathered. The police were called in and the stars' Rolls-Royce pulled up. A camera was set up inside the shop and filmed Ringo Starr striding up the High Street and into the shop. He looked around and then made for the counter, where "ticket salesman" John Lennon was standing. A large brightly-coloured poster advertising the Magical Mystery Tour covered a cigarette dispenser just to the left of the till. Ringo bought his tickets and left. End of scene, which was directed by Paul McCartney. Stan has fond memories of the experience, and so has his daughter, Penelope. Only seven then, she passed the time playing with John Lennon's moustache (the fake one he put on while playing the ticket salesman).

Two days later, on the Monday, the actors and camera crews were at West Malling airfield. Recollects, Tim Baldock of Baldocks Clothing Stores, West Malling, "There were flower painted cars and buses - and long-haired hippies in kaftans and sandals everywhere. The film crew wanted to shoot some crowd scenes, and we were recruited for the job. They directed us into a hangar where lights and scenery filled the place. Then the four came down a flight of stairs, miming a song which was being played over loudspeakers. Paul McCartney was directing the scenes and shouting orders all over the place."

Yet another local who remembers The Beatles visit is Peter Rimmer of Snodland. He was then a junior reporter on a local newspaper. "My attempt to interview George Harrison was brief and to the point," he recalls. "George just looked at me and said: 'Get a proper job'. End of interview!"

David Penny, a local schoolboy back then, played his part in the story of the Mystery Tour: "I'm the boy who falls over a fallen flag chasing some ballroom dancers about two minutes into the film. My father was sent to Aden with the RAF, so my mother and myself were sent to this virtually deserted station where The Beatles arrived to complete filming of the Magical Mystery Tour. My mother was asked if she and a few other wives could help with the washing-up in the catering vans. Within a day she was feeding The Fabs.

"I wasn't allowed to visit the site until the weekend. I arrived on the Friday evening just as the recruiting office scene was completed, and my mother told me that The Beatles had been gone for most of the day to the far end of the base by the blast walls filming 'I Am The Walrus'. Over the next two days I watched filming of the wizards' scenes, the coach races and Aunt Jessie's restaurant dream. On Saturday afternoon after feeding the crew and The Beatles their dinner my mother left the van leaving me with my lunch. Out of nowhere a face appeared at the hatch. 'Is there any more bread pudding please?' says Paul McCartney. 'No, I'm sorry there isn't,' says I. 'OK, thanks,' says Paul and off he goes. A Beatle had spoken to me."

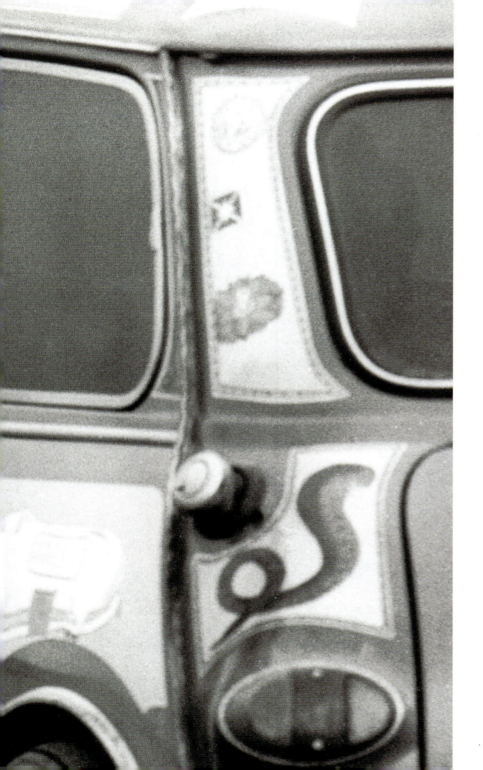

Victor Spinetti (actor): *"I'd worked with The Beatles in their previous movies, so John wrote to me and asked if I would be the courier in Magical Mystery Tour. I was busy doing a play, Oh What A Lovely War, in London, so I had to turn it down and Ivor Cutler went on and did it marvellously.*

But John still wanted me to be involved, so he got to me to drive down to West Malling Aerodrome for the day and do a little drill sergeant routine with Paul. It was something I did in the play anyway, and it was all improvised, so it was no problem.

One lovely thing was that when we broke for lunch, they had set aside twenty minutes for anybody who wanted to meditate, which I did. It was a lovely calm moment in the middle of the schedule, and they were all into that since they'd been with the Maharishi.

The filming was unusual inasmuch as it wasn't done in lots of short takes like a normal movie. They filmed long sequences, and they improvised as they went along. At one point John spotted a stuffed cow, and he just decided there and then to have it in the shot. They were making it up as they went along."

Rehearsing 'Your Mother Should Know' finale inside a hanger on West Malling air station Sunday 24th September with Peggy Spencer's Formation Dancing Team.

"My initial contact with The Beatles came through Denis O'Dell who was a friend of mine and worked on A Hard Day's Night and Help as executive producer. They wanted someone to edit the Magical Mystery Tour film they had shot and Denis suggested me. I was asked to go down and meet The Beatles at West Malling. Paul said, "We want to get this done in a week." I replied, "You have no chance ….if you see what's involved". They hadn't employed anyone to keep continuity notes and it was difficult to locate footage. Paul said, "Come and see the film, it's in Ringo's room". I went in and there was film everywhere, on top of the table, on top of the wardrobe, everywhere! The Beatles were viewing the daily rushes on Ringo's 16mm projector. They had three different types of film stock. Eventually they employed a secretary to make continuity notes and everything got sorted. When we got to the editing stage John and Paul would come in virtually everyday, we would work from about 10 in the morning until about 6 or 7 every night. They had many friends dropping into this little room in Old Compton Street, Soho. John employed a friend to go out and shoot any material he thought would be useful to include in the film, I cut some inserts into George's 'Blue Jay' Way sequence. Fans would drop in all day long and The Beatles would be very hospitable to them, but it was not getting the film edited. So I asked Paul to arrange for someone to be on the door so we could get on with job. So Mal Evans went on the door. They would ask me, 'Where are we eating today Roy?' We would go to a different restaurant or coffee house everyday. In the middle of editing they'd pop off to another room and meditate for 20 minutes, because they were into the Maharisha thing.

It took about a month to get to know John. He was really a shy person and you had to prove yourself to him before he decided to communicate. This came for me with the 'I Am The Walrus' number. We had only edited half the sequence when we realised there was not enough film shot to complete the song, as it was very long. So I said to John, 'Give me a couple of hours to work on it'. He looked at me almost disbelievingly and went away. I took out all the 'trims' of the film (the bits you don't use) and cut out all the visually interesting pieces, laying them into the most interesting visual movement of action. I then joined them together and synchronised them with the music to see the effect. At that point John returned, and both he and I were overjoyed that it worked so well. For John though, his emotions were only in a knowing nod and smile. But I knew that I had captured his respect.

Incidentally the starbursts you see at a couple of different intervals in the film were put there to cover the possibility of us having to break for commercial advertisements in the film. After the Magical Mystery Tour was virtually completed John wanted to use some of the unused footage for a full colour promo film for 'Hello Goodbye', so we put together about three minutes of film which included the luncheon at the Atlantic Hotel, footage shot in Nice etc. To this day the film has never been seen.

We had two machines going at the same time, one 16mm for MMT and another 35mm for the 'Hello Goodbye' promos and I needed to get MMT finished. So I said rather abruptly 'I must get MMT finished before we can start work on the promos. They were all taken aback for a moment and John wrote on the editing bench 'Roy freaked out today'…...!!!!! Eventually I got all the sequences from the Magical Mystery together, they couldn't believe they could get a film out of it, The Beatles were amazed. It was running for about 1 hour 15 minutes and I edited down to 52 minutes.

Some months later I received a call on a Friday evening from the Apple office asking me to go over to Abbey Road as Paul wanted to talk with me. When I arrived all The Beatles were there putting down tracks for their next album. I sat down with Paul in a corner and he explained that they wanted to shoot a promo for 'Hey Jude'. I had heard the song some weeks earlier and was really knocked out by it. Paul said they would like me to direct it and they wanted to shoot it in a day. Knowing that the song was seven minutes long I said it would require two days to shoot that amount of screen time. The idea was to shoot The Beatles in a prison background. This was the only spec. I was given. So Paul gave me a copy of the song and I went away to work over the weekend on a specifically timed script with a shot by shot breakdown of the lyric, working on visually exciting images to make this a very unusual film. I wrote the sequences centring on each of The Beatles lifestyle, taking them through to old age, to fade out on each of them in a rocking chair, all wearing John Lennon glasses. I had already started pre-production on the Monday, and was in the Apple office with my producer, when Peter Brown came out to inform us that they had decided to shoot the promo on 'tape' instead of 'film' and it would be included in the David Frost show. I argued, 'Is there anything I can do to change their minds?'. But alas 'no'. They have never seen the script I wrote, and I personally feel they missed a great opportunity to make a film that they could look back on in time and have something very special of 'their era'."

– ROY BENSON
MAGICAL MYSTERY TOUR FILM EDITOR

Magical Mystery Tour Fancy Dress Party

As a thank you The Beatles invited over 200 people, including the entire cast of The Magical Mystery Tour, the staff of NEMS and Apple and various relative and friends to a fancy dress party held at the Westbourne Suite of The Royal Lancaster Hotel, London, on the 21 December 1969. Paul and Jane came dressed as Pearly King and Queen; Ringo as a Regency buck and Maureen as an Indian princess; John as a rocker and Cynthia in Victorian costume whilst George sported an Errol Flynn outfit and Pattie looked great as an Eastern princess. Music was provided by The Chasers, The Symbols and The Dave Bartram Quintet not to mention The McPeake Family and The Bonzo Dog Doo Dah Band.

The Story of the
MAGICAL MYSTERY TOUR

Copyright © 1999 Tracks Ltd
This edition © 1999 Omnibus Press
(A Division of Book Sales Limited)

ISBN: 0.7119.7575.3
Order No: OP 48130

All rights reserved. No part of this book may be reproduced in any form or by any electronic or mechanical means, including information storage or retrieval systems, without permission in writing from the publisher, except by a reviewer who may quote brief passages.

Exclusive Distributors
Book Sales Limited,
8/9 Frith Street,
London W1V 5TZ, UK.

Music Sales Corporation,
257 Park Avenue South,
New York, NY 10010, USA.

The Five Mile Press,
22 Summit Road,
Noble Park,
Victoria 3174, Australia.

To the Music Trade only:
Music Sales Limited,
8/9 Frith Street,
London W1V 5TZ, UK.

Photo credits:
© Chris Walter/Photofeatures Cover shots and pages; 14, 15, 18, 19, 26, 34, 42.
© Hulton Getty pages; 1, 8, 10, 13, 16, 17, 39, 46, 48, 49, 50/51, 52 and shot on bookmark
© David Redfern/Redferns pages; 5, 22, 23, 24, 25, 27, 28, 29, 30, 32, 35, 38.
© Rex Features pages; 2, 3, 4.
© Tracks pages; 12, 20, 21, 30/31, 33, 36/37, 40, 43, 44, 45.

Text by Tony Barrow
Interview research by Johnny Black
With thanks to Julian Norton

Compiled by TRACKS LTD.

Every effort has been made to trace the copyright holders of the photographs in this book but one or two were unreachable. We would be grateful if the photographers concerned would contact us.

Printed in Singapore

A catalogue record for this book is available from the British Library.

Visit Omnibus Press on the web at www.omnibuspress.com